A Quiet Day

with the West

on Fire

A Quiet Day
with the West

on Fire

Poems

Margot Kahn

FLOATING
BRIDGE
PRESS

SEATTLE

A Quiet Day with the West on Fire is the finalist in the 2021 Floating Bridge Press chapbook competition.

©2021 Floating Bridge Press

ISBN 978-1-930446-09-0

Cover Design: Meghan McClure

Interior Layout: Michael Schmeltzer

The printing of this book was supported in part by grants from 4Culture, Allied Arts Foundation, and the Seattle Office of Arts & Cultural Affairs.

Floating Bridge Press
909 NE 43rd Street, #205
Seattle, Washington 98105
www.floatingbridgepress.org

Contents

A Quiet Day

with the West

on Fire

Walking to the End of the Road on the Last Day of July

This morning I found wild plums
growing at the end of the road beside the empty-
windowed barn, cool planets in a foliage galaxy.
And a white-haired woman riding a lawn mower
at the house with the red poppies,
next to the house of the summer people
with their concrete wall and metal fence,
their posted signs: Keep Out, KEEP OUT.

The tide is so low it's exposed islands
I've never seen, and tonight there'll be a black moon,
my father-in-law tells me. It's blackberry season.
All the way home I pluck the tender nubs
from their thorny vines wondering about the bay
beyond that wall, the water I imagine to be
more deserved, more pristine. What have I missed
in the time I've spent thinking about the things
I cannot see? How have I never noticed the plums
in all the years I've walked to the sea?

Exile

When everything's up in flames
I yearn for a yard I know the edge of,
for lightning bugs trapped in a punched-lid jar—

the lip of the brick fireplace where my father sang
his Navy songs, the kitchen where my mother's
blackberry pie bled out across the floor—

the days I drove myself to school and picked myself up,
hotwired the minivan, got felt-up and learned about loneliness
from a phone attached to the wall—

the place my parents were the first to be born to,
the place I had the privilege of being bored.
the place I had the privilege of leaving.

Here, from my kitchen window, the hills are first
to disappear. Then goes the fence, the garden,
the rutted gravel drive. Our lungs hurt just watching it,

reading in sans serif that friends had minutes to flee.
The hill behind their house awash in light, ablaze—
she posts it as they're rushing away

to the country of the displaced.
A land I know the scent of,
a language I, too, can speak.

Accidental Hosts

We fuck several times a week until
it gets tiresome and then we watch TV
or go to the movies. If the days

don't add up, we forget about it
for the month and drink with abandon.
No matter if we're supposed to stay away

from queso, street drugs and raw eggs. If
in those weeks our uterine linings
look thin or sad, it's not because we

haven't tried. But we wouldn't say we are
trying. When the baby is conceived
we'll drink only tea. If it's a ghost,

we'll lie down to hold it in until
we have to stand up, put our hands between
our legs and let it slip through our fingers

in the shower down the drain. If the twelfth
week comes and it's still there, we will make
phone calls and fill out paperwork. We

are not puppets or disciples. We don't want
to be cast out, marooned with a crib
in an empty room. We are accidental

hosts. We want to be what we've been—go
to the same job, the same bar, shoot the same
game of pool when our stomachs bulge over

the lip of the table. We are reviled,
derided, feared, and crowned. Yes, some fit
in their regular jeans for six months

and don't break out and still want sex, but look—
look at this thing we've done because we're
animals and we said *we'll see what happens*

until it actually happened and we
wondered what we'd done beyond logic
or reason in the light of the open door

peeling deli meat from the crisp paper
wrapping, folding it into our mouths.

Nordstrom Lingerie

Each pale pink box the salesgirl brings declares
these breasts were made by hand in Germany

and we take each one gingerly, hold them
like paper bags of produce to test the weight

and density, to notice the silicone creasing
like our sad, sagging skin. And suddenly we're

in our high school skins, palming faint nipples,
staring like we can't believe our luck.

What time this breast has lost, what touch—but for
the thousand women in that factory

who pass each breast from hand to hand, the way
you separate the raw yolk of an egg.

Do they work with music? Do they joke and chide?
Or do they cry with each slice of the knife?

If Someone Says Catalina

I think of this Janis Joplin
low-slung corduroy

cello-playing boy.
His gold hair swung

like a tiki bar curtain,
the fringe of a flapper dress

across my leg. Together
in a twin bed I was a window

and that hair was a shade
and the tassel, from my neck

to my navel, pulled itself down.
That boy played like nothing

I could afford—a twenty-year
whiskey on the rocks,

the melt of a glacier
pooled at my feet.

Now someone says Catalina
or cello or cancer

and I'm there again
singing over his requiem.

Tassel and tongue.
Shade and shroud.

Was it the hair, or the hands?
The sound, or the shape of the sound?

I'm saying this so that you
help me remember him.

So his mother knows
that night is accounted for.

On the Bus through Oregon

A banner of geese
unfurls, cut loose

from bolted storm
clouds. Stray snags

& burnt cartilage
erupt out of back-

yards, loneliness
jackknifed toward a

too-bright light.
A freight of peonies

goes north, aching
open & broken down.

In all other directions:
brushfire, burn piles.

I'm no one's mother
here, yarn around my

fingers, oranges
at my feet. But

I am a promise
of return: mother

as anecdote
to that lawn where

a hundred missiles
are arranged in lines,

aimed at nothing,
aimed at the sun.

A Quiet Day with the West on Fire

Upstairs, a boy hums while he plays.
Inside a Mason jar, a caterpillar rests
on the branch of a plum tree.
Cake sits on the counter. Bread cools.
A tomato ripens even as we hold our
breath waiting for the wind and rain.

We've asked ourselves the same question
a thousand times. I watch the caterpillar
sleep. I listen to the boy sing.
In these days of smoke and haze
I hold onto the smallest things—my fear
as suffocating as the open ocean, my heart
as boundless as the sky we used to know.

The World in My Phone and out the Window

California's in flames.
Hoar frost lights the fields.

Sexual misconducts tally on.
Fog rises off the water.

Containers wait to set sail.
There's snow all over Brooklyn.

Plovers skim across the Sound.
Logs are sorted for the saw.

A friend's daughter dances in Tel Aviv
barefoot, curly-haired, spinning.

My husband's message arrives: *Is your train on time?*
Someone I've never met has painted her nails red.

Western Story

Colt tied to the fence
broke its neck.
Goddamnit.
That's what you get, sometimes—
a wild one.

Winter

My husband and I get divorced
every winter, driving over the mountains.
It's like the joke about the chicken,
where the thing on the other side
is something worth getting to, only
the chicken is carrying the Talmud.
We'll be fine, says my husband.
But it's not us, I say,
that I'm worried about.
On the icy road we stop behind
a single-file line of cars.
While we wait, my son tiptoes
to the shoulder and pees.
The road is slick under packed snow,
dirty and deceptive, the way it was
when I was young and boys
would take me out in cars
late on winter nights, crank
the wheels and slam the brakes
in empty 4-ways, spinning us
like teacups at the county fair,
flesh into flesh, careening close
to tree trunks and telephone poles,
our tires leaving great, looping,
Spirograph tracks we'd get out
and admire, howling
into the stale suburban night.

When we push north,
we pass the accident—
the van on its roof, the driver's
side smashed in. The dull wail
of the ambulance coming down valley,
its sad song made soft by the snow.
My grandfather believed god chose him
to survive the Holocaust so he would father
a son. But I am my mother's daughter
and I have no such hubris. I'm here
by dumb luck and despite this foolishness.
It's the world outside
that's impossible to control,
every damn molecule bonding
and breaking without telling you.
But I trusted those boys the way I trust
my husband, his steady hands—
because I have to.

Field of Vision

Feathery as a frayed hem,
in the wind the hay field moves
like the tufted manes of a thousand
horses running. No—it moves
like the pleated skirts of a thousand girls
swishing as they walk to school.
After school, there was a girl's field
we'd crouch down in, curl and shiver
like fawns as someone's legs passed by
so close it seemed impossible
they'd miss you. They were tortures
in equal measure: the waiting
and the being found. From the edges
of that field, the girl's father whistled—
a whistling tune and another sound
that brought the children running
sharp as sheep dogs from the hay field
or the fronds of the willow tree or the far
fence we'd half-climb to watch the horses
in the neighbor's field, pretending
they were ours. Last week at the post office,
the tellers could barely be heard
over the thousand chicks cheeping
in cardboard boxes behind the counter.
Their feathery non-feathers. Their cheeps
of being young in a strange place
with only a small hole to see through.

I didn't do well in school
but I have come to understand
that a bond is only as strong as a breath
of air. When I learned that girl
no longer speaks to her father,
I thought of her room strung up
with 4-H ribbons, their blue and red tails
fluttering against a floral wall.
And when my son crawls into bed
whimpering a fetal cry, broken by
his parents not understanding him
for the first time, I am tender.
The hay will be cut tomorrow.
The raptors will come circling.
We'll watch from the shed roof,
where we can see the patterns
the mower cuts in the field.

Free Boat, No Trailer, at the Corner
of Kjargaard and Fisherman Bay

Yellowed tooth keeled to the cows, she's a boat
in a field not far from the sea. So you'd think

someone would want her. Water glimmers
in the distance. Cows graze the tender green.

Money hole. Joy ride. The mind sees
what it wants to remember: cold envelope

of the ocean. Traps lowered to unlit depths.
Who was she before she got here? Who

was I? What if you took everything you owned
and looked at it against a bareback sky?

I like that I'm a woman who can still
be curious when she turns a corner.

The boat has become a page of the field
that rewrites itself every season.

The Towels

Above the clawfoot tub they drape
the way the user draped them:

my husband's stretched across two hooks
the way a certain kind of man takes up space;

my son's hung up as in entangled,
the way we'd say a foot is caught in a stirrup

when the rider has gone down; and mine—
the plush weight of itself

folding over. I take them, bundled
in my arms, ten thousand fiber fingers

that go to the places I do not or
can no longer go: the crease of my son's thigh

where a mole like a button I want to press
grows, and all the crannies of my husband

I still wish to ravish.
I clutch them the way my grandmother

bundled and carried me to bed
where the towel unfurled at my feet

like the loosed petal of a spent flower—
the way she said the rotten clothes fell

from our cousins' bodies
when the soldiers came to free them.

Skiing

We put our feet in the twin tracks
and go where it's easier to admit
how much we don't always love our children.

We love our children the way the snow
piles on fence posts, the way the plow
comes to clear the drive. We love them

the way the dog bounds away and returns,
ice clinging to its chest, ice frozen
in its paws, hurting. We love our children

and we don't love them, a thing we can't say
unless we're out here where the tree
with the yellow bark is sending its shooters

to the sky, each branch holding a hundred kids
with pistols, arms held high—
and the snow's doing that thing it does

lolling over the lips of things like a dog's tongue,
ice dripping off smooth edges like saliva.
The snow lets our feet slip away from the house

and along the river that's saving breath
for itself. We ski past the country store,
past the warming hut, deeper and deeper

into the trees, wondering
how the river feels in spring,
when the ice melts, turns into river.

The Cleaner

Years ago, I hired a woman to help me clean
and she would text me during the week
when she was able to come, in between
her other jobs that were haphazard
and unpredictable. Her job that paid real
money was for the city: when there was a body—
a crime scene—she was the one who cleaned it.
And she loved this job, she told me. She loved
knowing which way the bullets flew
and with what velocity the body shattered.
She'd come to my house with Q-tips
and cleaning supplies she'd made by hand
and tell me everything while I held my baby:
The way blood decorates a wall. How far
splintered bone can travel. The way scraps
of fat and tissue settle into thick carpet,
how to pluck them out with tweezers.
One week it was a man who shot himself
in the basement. One week a 17-year-old
who hung himself in the garage.
Someone found them
and then someone called her—
my cleaner—to make it disappear
so that when the mother of that boy came home
she wouldn't find a drop of him—
not a vestige of his smell, not a scrap
of bitten fingernail. Which makes me wonder

what that mother thought would become of her boy
when her boy was young. Or what I might feel,
seven years from now, if my son
were to leave this world by his own hand.
Today on the toilet while I pee,
I stare at the hair on the floor where
my husband gave my son a trim
and wonder if I should keep it—
this clipping that escaped the broom.

Cold Creek

These are the last days of spring snow.
We take advantage by strapping on skis
and going out Cold Creek where the fir trees
drop bridal veils as we pass beneath,
as if we're being given.

I read that the Germans have a word
for forest solitude, and another
word for forest obscurity.
Do they have a word for crossing a bridge?
For the feeling in your arms and legs
when you have, possibly, ventured too far?
Do they have a word for the tracks
a small creature has dimpled in the snow,
the empty pockets of shadow?

At the warming hut, the wood stove's heat
shimmers and yawns. Someone offers
hot buttered rum steaming in a steel cup,
cheese and crackers, sweet, dried mango
that sticks in the crannies of our teeth.
On the way back, our knees will ache.
Make it burn, I'll say, and we'll laugh
about it, the aching.

A snowfield embraces snow the way
a body makes room for another body,

or a small-footed fox can tunnel
through the milky ducts of your breast.
Is there a word for the living thing
that was once here and now is not?
The wind and sun will take care
of its footsteps. In my mind
it will forever be running,
cold-footed, away from me.

On a Spring Sunday, I Forget My Wedding Ring

and, walking up the hill to the house
of my friend, my naked fingers rub
against each other, conscious of that
unarmored skin. My friend stood beside
me when I married, and I stood beside
my friend, and before that we slept
in the same bed laughing about nothing things,
like the fact of whales being mammals
and certain tight garments shimmering.
Now I am carrying meatballs in a plastic bag
because, while looking into the face
of uncertainty, my friend must eat.
And while I am walking, a man half my age
passes on the sidewalk and I'm delighted
by how my body sings—it thrums as throaty
a song as the warblers in the soft-lipped
magnolia trees. Perhaps if I hadn't
forgotten my wedding ring where I left it
on the counter while mixing the meat,
that man wouldn't have smiled and I wouldn't
have something to laugh about with my friend
when I hold her close, our breasts pressed together
as young and alive as we'll ever be.

Western Tanager

Arriving in woodlands in the middle of May,
he's red-headed and yellow-cloaked—dashing!

And you, wearing your new breast, your legs
iridescent like a hummingbird, your head

as bare as our babies' were, those tender skulls
in the palms of our hands—you're paler now.

Soon the children will be sent away and you'll
burn and peel and burn. Summer's churn.

By November this joule of a bird will have flown,
dressed as he is for the swim-up bar. But today

we were stopped on our path—breathless.

On Dissolution

Behind the barn
the blackberries crowd
around the water tank,
climb the west wall,
take back the field
along the fence line.
Picked and brought inside,
we muddle them with mint,
shake them with lemon
and spirits, pour it all
into pint jars, and take
sweet-bitter sips
while the swallows—
bank, barn, rough-
winged, violet green—
come barnstorming.
They glide in circles
or close to the ground,
slip through the hayloft doors,
through the gaping holes
in the roof and walls
that the wind opens wider
each winter without remorse.
This we agree is one solution
to dissolution:
abide in this place
though it is dark

and dismantling,
alight in the places
that will hold you,
pass through it with
the swiftest grace.

Fermata

Do you know what that means? said my son, kicking his legs
beneath the piano keys. His arms outstretched don't yet reach
the lowest A or the highest C, but at least he's learning.

In my grandparents' living room I tinkered, never taught,
while my grandmother lit candles for everyone she'd lost.
There, the old people kept the old country to themselves.

Here, the old people lift a finger or two off the steering wheel,
sometimes a whole hand. When I take a turn I hesitate,
questioning whether the wave or the road is more important.

When I was my son's age, my grandmother put a knife
through her palm trying to separate a pair of frozen steaks.
She called for help calmly, as if announcing a five-spade hand.

Earlier today, when a splinter lodged under my son's nail,
I pretended not to know the split of skin or the hurt of severing
so that he might bravely sing me his own song of cleaving.

Acknowledgments

Thank you to the editors of the following publications, in which these works, or earlier versions of them, first appeared:

Crab Creek Review:	"On Dissolution," "The Towels," & "Winter"
Grist:	"Fermata"
Jabberwock Review:	"The World in My Phone and out the Window"
New England Review:	"Field of Vision"
New Ohio Review:	"Exile"
Nimrod:	"Cold Creek"
Poetry Northwest:	"Nordstrom Lingerie" & "On a Spring Sunday, I Forget My Wedding Ring"
Pontoon:	"Accidental Hosts" & "Western Story"
Portland Review:	"A Quiet Day with the West on Fire"
San Antonio Review:	"If Someone Says Catalina"
Taproot:	"Walking to the End of the Road on the Last Day of July"

"Western Story" is anthologized in *Evergreen: Grim Tales & Verses from the Gloomy Northwest* (Scablands Books, 2021).

Thank you to Jericho Brown for selecting "Winter" as the winner of the *Crab Creek Review* 2019 Poetry Prize.

Thank you to Washington State's Artist Trust and King County's 4Culture for supporting this work with individual artist grants in 2019 & 2020. Thank you to Hugo House, where I learned to write a poem, and to my most generous teachers there: Keetje Kuipers, Ellen Bass, Rick Barot, Ed Skoog, Tess Taylor, Elizabeth Austen, Luther Hughes, and Erin Malone. Thank you to everyone who read these poems and made them better, especially: Rebecca Clarren, Sonya Schneider, John Okrent, Katie Prince, Kim Kent, Dujie Tahat, and Seth Rosenbloom. Special thanks to Laura Read, whose book, *Dresses from the Old Country*, so inspired me, and for her attention to an early draft of this manuscript. Thanks to Erin Malone for the wise edits and visionary reorder.

To Michael Schmeltzer, Rachel Mehl, Emilie Rommel Shimkus, and Makena Schoene — thank you for choosing this manuscript and giving it such generous care and attention.

Thanks most of all to my family for putting up with my refrigerator magnets and my stacks of books, and especially to Toby for saying, "Let's write a poem, Mommy!"

About the Author

Author Photo: Mary Grace Long

Margot Kahn is the author of the biography *Horses That Buck*, winner of the High Plains Book Award, and co-editor of the anthology *This Is the Place*, a *New York Times Book Review* Editors' Choice. Her essays and reviews have appeared in *The Rumpus, Lenny Letter, The Los Angeles Review, BUST,* and *Publishers Weekly,* among other places. Winner of the *Crab Creek Review* 2019 Poetry Prize and finalist for Palette Poetry's 2019 Emerging Poet Prize, her poems have appeared in *Poetry Northwest, New England Review, Tinderbox Poetry Journal, New Ohio Review,* and elsewhere. Margot earned an MFA from Columbia University and has been supported by the Seattle Office of Arts & Culture, 4Culture and ArtistTrust. She's currently at work on a new biography, *Until Tomorrow,* and a forthcoming anthology, *Wanting* (Catapult 2023).

About the Press

Floating Bridge Press is a 501(c)(3) nonprofit literary arts organization   founded in 1994. Our mission is to recognize and promote the work of poets in Washington State and beyond through publications and readings. Our board of directors and editorial committee are composed of volunteers from across the community.

Ask for our books at your local bookstore, or you can visit us online at *www.floatingbridgepress.org*.

Winners of the Floating Bridge Press
Chapbook Award

2021	Judith Skillman	*Oscar the Misanthropist*
2020	Brenda Miller	*The Daughters of Elderly Women*
2019	Katrina Roberts	*Lace*
2018	Natasha Kochicheril Moni	*A Nation (Imagined)*
2017	Katy E. Ellis	*Night Watch*
2016	Kate Peterson	*Grist*
2015	Michael Schmeltzer	*Elegy/Elk River*
2014	John Whalen	*Above the Pear Trees*
2013	Hannah Faith Notess	*Ghost House*
2012	Jodie Marion	*Another Exile on the 45th Parallel*
2011	Casey Fuller	*A Fort Made of Doors*
2010	Laura Read	*The Chewbacca on Hollywood Boulevard Reminds Me of You*
2009	Katharine Whitcomb	*Lamp of Letters*
2008	Nancy Pagh	*After*
2007	Holly J. Hughes	*Boxing the Compass*
2006	Annette Spaulding-Convy	*In the Convent We Become Clouds*
2005	Timothy Kelly	*Toccata & Fugue*
2004	Michael Bonacci	*The Former St. Christopher*
2003	Kelli Russell Agodon	*Geography*
2001	Joseph Green	*The End of Forgiveness*
2000	Chris Forhan	*X: A Poem*
1999	Bart Baxter	*Sonnets from the Mare Imbrium*
1998	Molly Tenenbaum	*Blue Willow*
1997	Donna Waidtlow	*A Woman Named Wife*
1996	Nance Van Winckel	*A Measure of Heaven*
1995	Joannie Kervran	*A Steady Longing of Flight*